Shaikh's Answers On DIFFERENT TOPICS

HOW SHAIKH 'ABD AL-QADIR RESPONDED TO QUESTIONS ON VARIOUS IMPORTANT TOPICS.

by Shaikh Muhammad ibn Yahya at-Tadifi al-Hanbalion

KITAB BHAVAN
New Delhi - 110 002 (INDIA)

KITAB BHAVAN
Publishers, Distributors, Exporters & Importers
1784, Kalan Mahal, Darya Ganj,
New Delhi - 1100 02 (India)

Phones	:	(91-11) 23277392/93, 23274686, 32906494
Fax	:	(91-11) 23263383
Website	:	www.nusratalinasri.com
	:	www.kitabbhavan.com
Email	:	nasri@vsnl.com
	:	nusrat@bol.net.in

Name of the book : Shaikh's Answers On Different Topics
Written by : Shaikh Abdul Qadir Jilani
Translated by : Shaikh Muhammad Ibn Yahya at-Tadifi al-Handbalion

1st Edition : 2011

ISBN : 81-7151-391-3

Printed & Published in India by :
Nusrat Ali Nasri for KITAB BHAVAN
1784, Kalan Mahal, Darya Ganj,
New Delhi - 1100 02 [India]

CONTENTS

CONCERNING DIVINELY-INSPIRED RECEIVINGS [MAWARID ILAHIYYA] AND SATANIC INSINUATIONS [TAWARIQ SHAITANIYYA].

Shaikh 'Abd al-Qadir (may Allah be well pleased with him) was asked to explain the distinctive characteristics of Divinely-inspired receivings [mawarid Ilahiyya] and satanic insinuations [tawariq shaitaniyya]. He replied:

"The Divinely-inspired receiving comes only in response to an appeal [istid'a']. It does not go away because of any intervening cause [sabab]. It does not come in one particular mode [namat], nor at any specific time. As for the satanic insinuation [tariq shaitani], it is contrary to that in all respects."

CONCERNING LOVE [MAHABBA].

When asked about love [mahabba], the Shaikh (may Allah be well pleased with him) said: "It is a disturbance [tashwish] that affects the heart. It is inspired by the Beloved [Mahbub], by contrast with Whom this world comes to be like the ring of a seal, or a funeral wake. Love is an intoxication that has no corresponding sobriety. It is total devotion to the Beloved, in every respect, both in private and in public, with a self-effacing predilection. It is a natural impulse, not an affectation.

"Love is blindness to everything other than Beloved, due to solicitude for Him. It is also blindness to the Beloved Himself, due to a profound respect for Him. It is therefore total blindness. Lovers [muhibbun] are too drunk to get sober, except through direct vision of the Beloved. They are too sick to be cured, except by the sight of the One they seek. They are too distressed to be consoled, except by their Master [Mawla]. They can find no refuge, except in the remembrance of Him. They do not respond to anyone, except to His summoner."

"As Majnun [the crazy lover of] Layla put it:

My relatives all blame me for loving Layla:

my brother, my cousins, my aunt...."

(The rest of the verses are well known, so there is no need to spell them out here.)

CONCERNING THE REALIZATION OF DIVINE ONENESS [TAWHID].

When the Shaikh (may Allah be well pleased with him) was asked about the realization of Divine Oneness [tawhid], he said:

"[It is signified by] the indications of the secret of consciences [dama'ir], and of the hidden content of the secret of the innermost beings [sara'ir], at the advent of the Divine Presence [Hadra]. [It is signified by] the passage of the heart beyond the ultimate boundary of thoughts, its elevation to the highest degrees of connection [wisal], its penetration of the veils of glorification, its progress toward nearness on the feet of detachment, its advance toward proximity with the effort of singular devotion, in combination with the annihilation of the two realms of being, the vacating of the two domains [this world and the Hereafter], the removal of the two sandals, the acquisition of the two lights, and the extinction of all the worlds beneath the radiance of the lights of the brilliant flashes of disclosure, without previous intention."

CONCERNING DETACHMENT [TAJRID].

In answer to a question concerning detachment [tajrid], the Shaikh (may Allah be well pleased with him) explained:

"It is the detachment of the innermost being [sirr] from the consideration of ways and means [tadabbur], by steadily restraining it from pursuit of the object of desire, by stripping it bare, then clothing its nakedness with the assurance of freedom from restriction, and by returning from the creation [khalq] to the Truth [Haqq], in a state of repentance."

CONCERNING DIRECT KNOWLEDGE [MA'RIFA].

When the Shaikh (may Allah be well pleased with him) was asked about knowledge acquired by direct experience [ma'rifa], he said:

"It is insight into the meanings of the secrets of the hiding places of the mysteries, and recognition of the visible signs of the Lord of Truth [Haqq] in everything that exists, by viewing every element thereof in the light of the meanings of His Uniqueness [Wahdaniyya]. It is the acquisition of the knowledge of Reality [Haqiqa] in the extinction of every transitory being, when the Everlasting [Baqi] points toward it with the sign of the awe-inspiring dignity of Lordship [Rububiyya]. It is recognition of the trace of perpetuity [baqa'] in what the Everlasting [Baqi] has indicated, in the light of the majesty of Divinity [Ilahiyya], by looking with the eye of the heart."

CONCERNING SPIRITUAL ASPIRATION [HIMMA].

When someone asked him about spiritual aspiration [himma], the Shaikh (may Allah be well pleased with him) explained:

"It means that the aspirant becomes completely naked, in every part of his being. In the case of his lower self [nafs], it is stripped of the love of this world. In the case of his spirit [ruh], it is stripped of attachment to the Hereafter. In the case of his heart [qalb], it is stripped of any will that competes with the Will of the Master [Mawla]. As for his innermost being [sirr], it is detached from paying the slightest attention to the created universe, even with a quick peep or a glance."

CONCERNING THE HIGHEST OF ALL THE DEGREES OF DIVINE REMEMBRANCE [DHIKR].

When the Shaikh (may Allah be well pleased with him) was asked about the highest of all the degrees of Divine remembrance [dhikr], he said:

"It is that which impresses the heart, by command of the Lord of Truth (Almighty and Glorious is He) at the moment of His choice, with the perpetuity of everlasting providence ['inaya]. This remembrance [dhikr] is permanent, persistent and enduring. No trace of forgetfulness impairs it, and no heedlessness disturbs it, for the feelings, instincts and thoughts are all involved in the act of remembering. This is the frequent remembrance [dhikr kathir] referred to by the Lord of Truth (Glory be to Him, and Exalted is He) in His revelation.144 The best kind of remembrance is that which is prompted by the signals received from the All-Compelling Sovereign [al-Malik al-Jabbar], in the recesses of our innermost beings [asrar]."

CONCERNING ARDENT YEARNING [SHAWQ].

When someone asked him about ardent yearning [shawq], the Shaikh (may Allah be well pleased with him) explained:

"The best of all ardent yearnings [ashwaq] is that which is stimulated by witnessing [mushahada], for it never wearies of meeting, never tires of telling, never flags because of closeness, and never fades because of intimacy. On the contrary, the more the contact is experienced, the more ardent the yearning becomes."

"Ardent yearning cannot be truly authentic, until it is completely stripped of its deficiencies: namely, the influence of an underlying motive, the pursuit of an ambitious desire, or the protection of a selfish interest. It thus becomes an ardent yearning stripped of all secondary causes [asbab]. The person concerned has no idea what makes him feel the way he feels, because he is always witnessing the object of his yearning, yet he still yearns for the witnessing thereof, however much that witnessing is experienced."

CONCERNING ABSOLUTE TRUST [TAWAKKUL].

When someone asked him about absolute trust [tawakkul], the Shaikh (may Allah be well pleased with him) explained:

"It is the preoccupation of the innermost being [sirr] with Allah (Exalted is He), to the exclusion of any other than Him. When someone puts all his trust in the Lord, he forgets whatever he used to rely on, for His sake, and depends on Him entirely, to the exclusion of all apart from Him. He thereby ascends from the shame of nonentity [fana'] to the state of absolute trust."

"Absolute trust [tawakkul] is the raising of the glance of the eye of direct perception [ma'rifa], by the innermost being [sirr], toward the hidden mystery of things decreed by destiny [maqdurat]. It is the firm belief, based on the reality of certainty [haqiqat al-yaqin], in the concepts grasped by the methods of direct perception, because they are sealed [with the stamp of Truth], and therefore immune to the opposite of certainty."

In answer to another question concerning absolute trust [tawakkul], the Shaikh (may Allah be well pleased with him) explained:

"Absolute trust [tawakkul] is a reality [haqiqa] like the reality of sincere devotion [ikhlas]. The reality of sincere devotion is the transfer of the aspiration [himma] from the rewards [obtained by deeds] to the deeds [themselves]. The same is true of absolute trust, since it is the abandonment of personal power and strength, in favour of reliance on the Lord of lords [Rabb al-arbab] (Glory be to Him, and Exalted is He)."

Then he went on to say (may Allah be well pleased with him):

"O young man! How often you are spoken to, but do not hear! How often you hear, but fail to understand! How often you understand, but do not take action! How often you take action, but do not act sincerely, and do not become immersed in your sincere devotion, with your whole being!"

CONCERNING CONTRITION [INABA].

When the Shaikh (may Allah be well pleased with him) was asked about contrition [inaba], he said:

"Contrition is the effort to pass beyond the intermediate stations, and to beware of halting on the ascending stages; then to advance to the highest of the hidden levels, and to focus the aspirations on the occurrence of the sessions of the Presence [majalis al-Hadra]; then to return entirely to the Lord of Truth (Glory be to Him, and Exalted is He), after being present in the place of Presence, and witnessing this confrontation [muhadara]. Contrition [inaba] means returning to Him from Him, for safety's sake [hadharan], and returning to Him from everything other than Him, in hopeful anticipation [raghaban], and returning to Him from every attachment, in fearful apprehension [rahaban]."

CONCERNING REPENTANCE [TAWBA].

When someone asked him about repentance [tawba], the Shaikh (may Allah be well pleased with him) explained:

"Repentance is the process whereby the Lord of Truth (Exalted is He) looks toward His ancient and predestined providence ['inaya] for His servant, directs that providence toward His servant's heart, and tenderly detaches it, by attracting it toward Him and grasping it. When this takes place, the heart is drawn toward Him, away from corrupt ambition. The spirit obediently complies, the heart and the mind follow suit, repentance [tawba] is truly accomplished, and the whole affair becomes proper to Allah (Exalted is He)."

CONCERNING THIS WORLD [AD-DUNYA].

In response to a question concerning this world [ad-dunya], the Shaikh (may Allah be well pleased with him) said:

"Evict it from your heart into your hand, so that it cannot beguile you."

CONCERNING WEEPING [BUKA'].

When the Shaikh (may Allah be well pleased with him) was asked about weeping [buka'], he said:

"Weep for Him, weep because of Him, and weep over Him."

CONCERNING SUFISM [TASAWWUF].

When someone asked him about Sufism [tasawwuf], the Shaikh (may Allah be well pleased with him) explained:

"The Sufi is someone who makes that which the Lord of Truth wishes from him the object of his own wish. He renounces this world, so it serves him, and his allotted shares [aqsam] coincide with his needs. He achieves his purpose in this world, before the Hereafter, for his well-being is ensured by his Lord."

CONCERNING THE DIFFERENCE BETWEEN EXULTATION [TA'AZZUZ] AND ARROGANCE [TAKABBUR].

When the Shaikh (may Allah be well pleased with him) was asked to explain the difference between sheer exultation [ta'azzuz] and boastful arrogance [takabbur], he said:

"Sheer exultation [ta'azzuz] is taking pride for the sake of Allah, and in Allah. It entails the abasement of the lower self [nafs] and the raising of the aspiration [himma] toward (Exalted is He). As for boastful arrogance [takabbur], it is taking pride for the sake of the lower self, and in passionate desire. It entails the excitement of natural instinct, and the predominance of self-will, instead of respect for Allah (Almighty and Glorious is He). Natural pride is so much easier than pride that must be earned."

CONCERNING THANKFULNESS [SHUKR].

When someone asked him about thankfulness [shukr], the Shaikh (may Allah be well pleased with him) explained:

"The true nature of thankfulness [haqiqat ash-shukr] is the acknowledgment of the benefaction of the Benefactor [ni'mat al-Mun'im], with an attitude of humility, an overt recognition of the blessing, and a reverential confession of one's inability to give adequate thanks." Thankfulness can be subdivided into several categories, namely:

1. Thankfulness expressed by the tongue [shukr al-lisan]. This constitutes the acknowledgment of the benefaction [ni'ma] with an attitude of humble acceptance [istikana].

2. Thankfulness expressed by the body and the limbs [shukr bi'l-badan wa'l-arkan]. This is the characteristic indication of loyalty and readiness to serve [al-wafa' wa'l-khidma].

3. Thankfulness expressed by the inner feeling [shukr bi'l-qalb]. This requires a careful balance between the visible display of appreciation and the constant preservation of a sense of reverence.

"Beyond this stage, thankfulness passes from the realm of the visible to the realm of the invisible [ghaiba], where the focus of attention is the Benefactor [Mun'im], rather than the benefaction [ni'ma]."

"The person who is simply thankful [shakir] is someone who gives thanks for what is available [mawjud], while the person who is very thankful [shakur] is someone who gives thanks for what is unavailable [mafqud]."

"The person who gives praise [hamid] is someone who regards withholding as a gift, and views harm as a benefit, and in whose sight the two qualities eventually become equal."

"The glory [majd] that exhausts all expressions of praise [mahamid] is the witnessing of perfection [kamal], in the quality of Beauty [Jamal] and the attribute of Majesty [Jalal], with the eye of direct perception, on the carpet of nearness [to the Lord]."

CONCERNING PATIENCE [SABR].

In response to a question concerning patience [sabr], the Shaikh (may Allah be well pleased with him) said:

"Patience [sabr] means coping with misfortune by remaining on your best behaviour. It means welcoming His decrees, and accepting them in accordance with the statutes [ahkam] of the Book and the Sunna."

Patience [sabr] can be subdivided into several categories, namely:

1. Patience for the sake of Allah [sabr li'llah] (Exalted is He). This is the kind of patience [sabr] that is exercised in the course of carrying out His commandments and respectfully observing His prohibitions.

2. Patience in bearing with Allah [sabr ma'a'llah] (Exalted is He). This is the kind of patience [sabr] that is exercised by calmly enduring the effects of His decree and His actions within you, and by demonstrating indifference to the advent of poverty, without a scowl or a frown.

3. Patience in anticipation of Allah [sabr 'ala'llah] (Exalted is He). This is the kind of patience [sabr] that is exercised through steadfast reliance on that which He has promised, and that which He has threatened, in all things.

"The journey from this world to the Hereafter should be easy for the true believer [mu'min], but separation from creatures, even for love of the Truth, is difficult. The journey from what is known by hearsay [naqli] to [the direct experience of] Allah

(Exalted is He) is very hard, and patience in bearing with Allah [sabr ma'a'llah] is even more difficult."

"The patient pauper is worthier than the grateful rich man, and the grateful pauper is worthier than either. As for the pauper who is both patient and thankful, he is worthier than any of them."

"No one courts misfortune, with the exception of him who knows its spiritual reward."

CONCERNING GOODNESS OF MORAL CHARACTER [HUSN AL-KHULQ].

When someone asked him about goodness of moral character [husn al-khulq], the Shaikh (may Allah be well pleased with him) explained:

"What it signifies is that you are not affected by the rudeness of creatures [khalq], once you have become acquainted with the Truth [Haqq]. It means that you belittle your own lower self [nafs] and whatever arises from it, in full recognition of its faults. It means that you honour your fellow creatures, and what arises from them, by showing respect for what has been entrusted to them, in the way of faith and wisdom. That is the most excellent of all the virtues of the servant [of the Lord], and the jewels of the men of valour become manifest therein."

CONCERNING ACCEPTANCE [AKHDH] AND REJECTION [RADD].

When the Shaikh (may Allah be well pleased with him) was asked about the acceptance and rejection [of gifts and opportunities], he said:

"So long as passionate desire is present, voluntary acceptance is an act of wilfulness and discord. In the absence of passionate desire, on the other hand, acceptance is an act of compliance and concord, to refrain from which would amount to ostentation [riya'] and hypocrisy [nifaq]."

CONCERNING TRUTHFULNESS [SIDQ].

When someone asked him about truthfulness [sidq], the Shaikh (may Allah be well pleased with him) explained:

"There is truthfulness in words, and there is truthfulness in deeds, provided they are exposed to examination by the Lord of Truth (Glory be to Him, and Exalted is He). As for truthfulness in spiritual states, it is practiced by presenting to the Truth all the notions [khawatir] that occur, so that no outside influence can confuse them, and no remnant of doubt can challenge them."

CONCERNING PERSONAL EXTINCTION [FANA'].

In response to a question concerning personal extinction [fana'], the Shaikh (may Allah be well pleased with him) explained:

"It is experienced when the Lord of Truth discloses Himself to the innermost being [sirr] of His saint [wali], with a most immediate manifestation [tajalli]. Under the impact of that demonstration, the whole universe is annihilated, and the saint [wali] becomes extinct. The extinction [fana'] he thereby undergoes is actually his survival in perpetuity [baqa'], but he will only survive under the direction of the Everlasting One [Baqi], for it is He who has rendered him extinct, and it is He who has granted him perpetual existence."

CONCERNING SURVIVAL IN PERPETUITY [BAQA'].

When someone asked the Shaikh (may Allah be well pleased with him) about survival in perpetuity [baqa'], he said:

"It comes about only through the Meeting that is not accompanied by extinction [fana'], nor by separation. This only happens like the twinkling of the eye, or even more immediately. The mark of the people of perpetuity [ahl al-baqa'] is that nothing accompanies them in that capacity, because the two are opposites."

CONCERNING FULFILMENT OF DUTY [WAFA'].

In answer to a question concerning fulfilment of duty [wafa'], the Shaikh (may Allah be well pleased with him) explained:

"It is careful attention to the rights [huquq] of Allah (Exalted is He), even in deprivation, strict observance of the limits [hudud] set by Allah (Exalted is He), in word and in deed, and making haste to earn His good pleasure, in every situation, both in privately and in public."

CONCERNING CONTENTMENT [RIDA].

When someone asked the Shaikh (may Allah be well pleased with him) about contentment [rida], he said:

"It is the removal of the desire for favourable attention, satisfaction with whatever has been predestined in the foreknowledge of Allah (Exalted is He) in His eternity-without-beginning [azal], and contentment [rida] with what has been foreordained in destiny's decree [qadar]."

CONCERNING SELF-WILL [IRADA].

In response to a question concerning self-will [irada], the Shaikh (may Allah be well pleased with him) explained:

"It is the repetition of thought [fikr] within the heart [fu'ad]."

CONCERNING DIVINE PROVIDENCE ['INAYA].

When someone asked him about Divine providence ['inaya], the Shaikh (may Allah be well pleased with him) explained:

"It is sempiternal [azaliyya], for it is one of the Attributes [Sifat] of Allah (Exalted is He). He has not divulged it to anyone, and it cannot be reached by any device. It cannot be impaired by any means. No deficiency can corrupt it, and nothing can disrupt it. It is the secret of Allah (Exalted is He), kept in the presence of Allah. No one is privy to it, and the universe cannot find access to it."

"Divine providence ['inaya] is eternal, not temporal. Allah (Exalted is He) qualifies whomever He wills among His creatures as worthy to receive it. The mark of one who is worthy of Divine providence is captivity, then imprisonment, then confinement in chains, then being deprived by Him of all connection with creatures."

CONCERNING THE STATE OF ECSTASY [WAJD].

When someone asked him about the state of ecstasy [wajd], the Shaikh (may Allah be well pleased with him) explained:

"It is the state in which the spirit [ruh] is preoccupied with the sweetness of the remembrance [dhikr], and the lower self [nafs] is preoccupied with the pleasure of the entertainment [tatrib], while the innermost being [sirr] remains wholly devoted to the Beloved Friend [Habib], impervious to any outside influence, in its dedication to the Truth, in the presence of the Truth [Haqq]."

"The experience of ecstasy is a beverage which the Master [Mawla] gives his saint [wali] to drink, on the pulpit of His Noble Grace [Karama]. When he drinks, he becomes light-headed, and when he becomes light-headed, his heart flies on the wings of intimate friendship [uns] in the gardens of Holiness [Quds]. Then it falls into the ocean of awe, and is thrown into a trance, so the ecstatic [wajid] swoons into unconsciousness."

CONCERNING FEAR [KHAWF].

When someone asked the Shaikh (may Allah be well pleased with him) about fear [khawf], he said:

"There are several kinds of fear. There is the fear [khawf] that applies to those who are guilty of sin [mudhnibin]. There is the anxiety [rahba] that applies to those who practice worshipful service ['abidin]. There is the apprehension [khashya] that applies to the learned ['alimin]. There is the timidity [wajal] that applies to the lovers [muhibbin]. There is also the awe [haiba] that applies to those who know by direct experience ['arifin]."

"The fear experienced by sinners is the fear of the punishments that lie in store for them. The fear experienced by worshippers is due to [their uncertainty about] the spiritual reward of their acts of worshipful service. The fear experienced by the learned is the fear of committing shirk khafi [hidden association of partners with Allah] in their acts of worshipful obedience. The fear experienced by the lovers is the fear of missing the Meeting [with the Beloved]. The fear experienced by those who know by direct experience takes the form of awe and reverence [ta'zim], which is the most intense kind of fear, because it never fades away, whereas these other kinds do abate, when they are met with compassion and tender kindness."

CONCERNING HOPE [RAJA'].

In response to a question about hope [raja'], the Shaikh (may Allah be well pleased with him) explained:

"As far as the saints [awliya'] are concerned, hope means having a good opinion [husn az-zann] of Allah (Exalted is He). It has nothing to do with any desire for benefit, nor for the removal of harm, because those who are worthy of sainthood [ahl al-wilaya] know full well that He has taken care of all their needs. That knowledge makes them realize the value of personal extinction [fana']. To have a good opinion [of Allah] is therefore more meritorious than hope."

"Hope cannot exist without fear, because, if someone hopes to achieve something, he is bound to fear that it may escape him. To have a good opinion of Allah (Exalted is He) means recognizing Him in the beauty of His attributes [sifat], then basing your expectation [amal] of Him on what is relevant to Him, not on what relates to His servant. That expectation must be based on the knowledge that His attributes include Beneficent [Muhsin], Generous [Karim], Compassionate [Rahim], Gracious [Latif], and Kind [Ra'uf]."

"To have a good opinion of Allah (Exalted is He) means attaching your aspirations to previous experience of Divine providence ['inaya], and directing your heart toward the Lord, without arousing desire in the heart, and without exciting unduly optimistic feelings."

"The craving of the common folk has many valid causes, which entitle it to be dignified by the term 'hope [raja'],' but when most of those causes cease to provide its motivation, the term 'greed [tama']' is more appropriate to it than the term 'hope [raja'].'"

"Hope without fear is a sense of security [amn], while fear without hope is despair [qunut]."

"As the Prophet (Allah bless him and give him peace) once said:

If the fear of the true believer could be weighed, and his hope, the two would not be equal in weight."

CONCERNING THE SENSE OF SHAME [HAYA'].

When someone asked the Shaikh (may Allah be well pleased with him) about the sense of shame [haya'], he said:

"It means that the servant [of the Lord] feels too ashamed to say "Allah," so long as he has not fulfilled his duty to Him. It means that he turns toward Allah in unlawful situations, and that he does not appeal to Allah for anything to which he is not entitled. It means that he abandons acts of sinful disobedience out of shame, not from fear. It means that he duly performs all acts of worshipful obedience, aware that the Lord of Truth is watching over Him, so that he feels a sense of shame in His presence."

"The sense of shame [haya'] is engendered by the removal of the veil between the heart and the experience of awe [haiba]."

CONCERNING DIRECT WITNESSING [MUSHAHADA].

In response to a question concerning direct witnessing [mushahada], the Shaikh (may Allah be well pleased with him) explained:

"It is the experience of becoming blind to the two realms of being [this world and the Hereafter] with the eye of the heart, and beholding the Lord of Truth with the eye of direct perception [ma'rifa]. It means that the hearts acquire insight, through the pure vision of certainty [yaqin], into what He has told us about the invisible realms [ghuyub]."

CONCERNING NEARNESS [QURB].

When someone asked the Shaikh (may Allah be well pleased with him) about nearness [qurb], he said:

"It is the rolling up of distances by the grace of proximity [tayy al-masafat bi-lutf al-mudanat]."

CONCERNING SPIRITUAL INEBRIATION [SUKR].

When someone asked him about spiritual inebriation [sukr], the Shaikh (may Allah be well pleased with him) explained:

"It is the fermentation [ghalayan] of the hearts, brought about by the remembrance [dhikr] of the Beloved. Fear [khawf] is the disturbance of the hearts, induced by what they learn from the impact of the Beloved. Certainty [yaqin] is the verification of the causes and the secrets, through mastery of the transcendental mysteries, contact with the Beloved, separation from everything apart from Him, the cultivation of intimate familiarity, estrangement from external influences, and total absorption in remembrance [dhikr]."

"It means that you see yourself, in the state of remembrance, as completely absent from everything other than Him. It means that you abandon artificial respect in the state of direct witnessing, and pretended affection in the state of Meeting. Direct witnessing makes ordinary comprehension impossible, and total absorption in love is inconceivable by any stretch of the imagination."

"When the wish gathers strength, and the remembrance becomes connected with it, and the dedication becomes intense, love [mahabba] is engendered thereby. When the wish for Him envelops the heart, the whole of it becomes His possession. Then, when He has possessed it, the wish for anything other than Him falls from the heart, and the transfer of ownership becomes a reality. This is a pure state of being. When you remember Him, you are a lover [muhibb], and when you hear His remembrance of you, you are a loved one [mahbub]."

"Your fellow creatures are the veil that screens you from your own self [nafs], and your own self is the veil that screens you from your Lord [Rabb]."

"Poverty [faqr] is a kind of death, yet people try to enjoy life in it."

"Talk [qal] is what the common people are guided by, whereas the spiritual state [hal] is the source of guidance for the special few."

"When He sets you at ease, a state of relaxation is experienced. Your dispensation [rukhsa] is converted into strict observance ['azima], then your strict observance is converted into playfulness [dalal]. Dispensation is for those who are lacking in faith [iman]. Strict observance is for those whose faith is perfect. Sovereignty [mulk] is for those who are personally extinct [fanin]."

CONCERNING THE MEANING OF THE TERM "[SPIRITUAL] PAUPER" [FAQIR].

When someone asked the Shaikh (may Allah be well pleased with him) about the meaning of the term "[spiritual] pauper" [faqir], he said: "[In the Arabic script, it is written with the letters]: fa'-qaf-yay-ra'." Then he explained the significance of each of these letters in poetic verse:

The initial fa' of the faqir stands for his absorption [fana'] in his essence, and his detachment [faragh] from his description and his attributes.

fa'u'l-faqiri fana'u-hu fi dhati-hi-wa faraghu-hu min na'ti-hi wa sifati-h.

The qaf stands for the strength [quwwa] of his heart in [its dedication to] his Beloved, and his commitment [qiyam] to Allah for the sake of His good pleasure.

wa'l-qafu quwwatu qalbi-hi bi-Habibi-hi-wa qiyamu-hu li'llahi fi mardati-h.

The yay shows that he pins his hope [yarju] on Him, and fears [yakhafu] Him, and performs [yaqumu] his duty as true devotion demands.

wa'l-yayu yarju bi-hi wa yakhafu-hu-wa yaqumu bi't-taqwa bi-haqqi tuqati-h.

The ra' stands for the refinement [riqqa] of his heart and its purity, and its return [ruju'] to Allah from its carnal desires.

wa'r-ra'u riqqatu qalbi-hi wa-safa'u-hu-wa ruju'u-hu li'llahi 'an shahawati-h.

The Shaikh (may Allah be well pleased with him) then went on to say:

"What is required of the spiritual pauper [faqir] is that he should be flexible in thinking [fikr] and centred in remembrance [dhikr], courteous in disagreement [munaza'a] and ready to assist in reconciliation [muraja'a]. He must seek nothing from the Lord of Truth but the Truth [Haqq], and he must practice nothing but truthfulness [sidq]. He must be the most tolerant of people, and the most self-effacing. His laughter should be of the cheerful, smiling kind, and his curiosity should be used as an instrument of learning. He should be a reminder to the heedless, and a teacher to the ignorant. He must not hurt those who hurt him, and he must not meddle in things that do not concern him."

"He must give plenty in the way of favours, but little in the way of offence. He must be careful to abstain from things that are unlawful, and stand well clear of things that are of dubious legality [shubuhat]. He must be a helper [ghawth] to the stranger, and a father to the orphan. His joy should be apparent in his face, while his sadness is stored in his heart. He should be engrossed in his contemplation [fikr] and happy in his poverty [faqr]. He must not disclose a secret, nor rend a veil. He must be graceful in movement, bountiful in kindness, charming in outlook, generous in providing benefits, refined in taste, excellent in moral character, and very gentle."

"He should be a precious substance that melts and flows. He should be long on silence [samt], agreeable in manner [na't], forbearing when he is treated foolishly, and very patient with anyone who treats him badly. There should be no freezing [jumud] of the feelings in his presence, and no extinguishing [khumud] of the fire of Truth. He must never be slanderous [nammum], envious [hasud], impetuous ['ajul], or malicious [haqud]. He must treat the elderly with deference, and the young with compassion."

"He must be worthy of trust [amana] and far from betrayal [khiyana]. His habit should be true devotion, and modesty should be his natural disposition. He should always be on the alert, and make vigilance his constant practice. He should take little for granted, and be very long-suffering. He should mean little to himself, but a great deal to his brothers. His behaviour should be an example of good conduct [adab], and his speech should be a marvel ['ajab]. He must never gloat over anyone's misfortune, nor speak ill of anyone behind his back."

"He must be dignified and very patient, content and very thankful. He should spend little time in talking, and make a frequent practice of ritual prayer [salat] and fasting. He must be truthful of tongue, and steadfast of heart. He should treat his guests with cordial hospitality, and supply everyone present with whatever food is available. When disasters befall him, his neighbours must not be adversely affected."

"He must not be a verbal abuser [sabbab], a backbiter [mughtab], a slanderer [ghayyab], a calumniator [nammam], or a fault-finder [dhammam]. He must not be impetuous ['ajul], inattentive [ghaful], envious [hasud], irritable [malul], malicious [haqud], or ungrateful [kanud]."

"He must have a tongue that is stored away [makhzun], a heart that is grief-stricken [mahzun], a way of speaking that is measured [mawzun], and a way of thinking that travels far and wide, through what has been and what is yet to be [ma yakun]."